Finish the words.

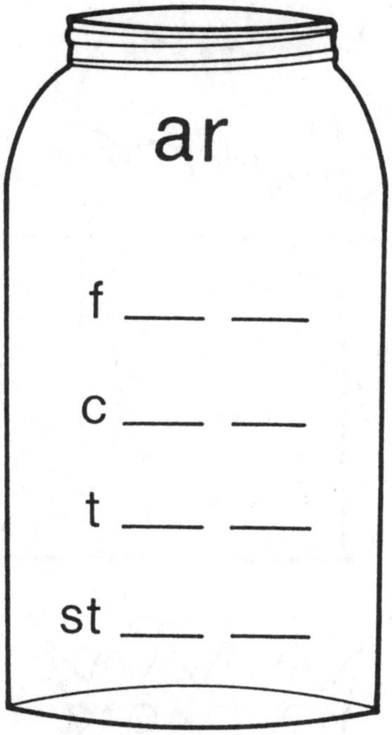

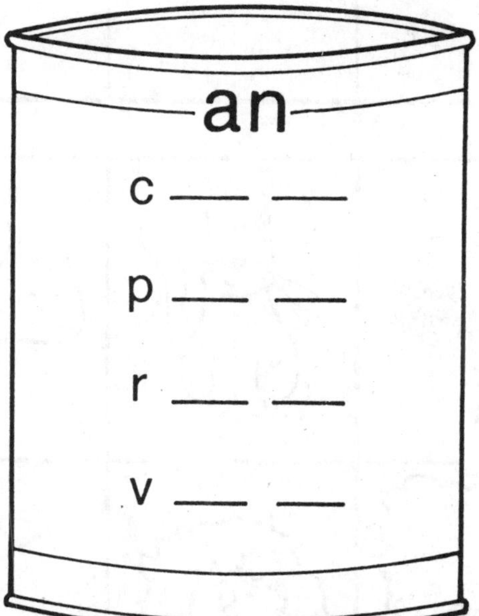

Cut and paste the pictures that rhyme.

3

Fill in the blank with a rhyming word.

1. A big green frog __________
sat on a __log__ .

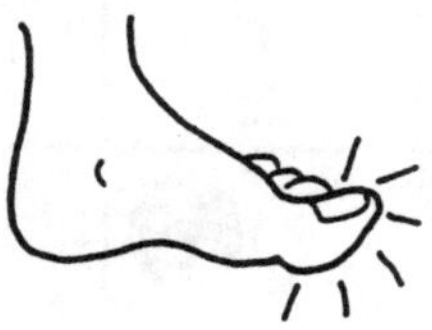

2. I hit my **toe** __________
with the __________ .

3. My sister's **cat** __________
sat on Dad's __________ .

4. The little **bee** __________
buzzed around the __________ .

Color the words that rhyme with **at**.

bug	can	dog	den pat	let
big bat	hop fat	jam hat	slat	fun cat
mat vat	splat	Nat	at	that
sat met	Pat fox	flat get	brat	rat nap
pot	win	man	tat run	bed

I see a ________________.

Fill in the missing words.

1. It is ____________ to ____________ in the ____________.

sun	fun	run

2. ____________ put grape ____________ on his ____________.

ham	jam	Sam

3. ____________ has a big ____________ ____________.

red	Fred	sled

4. Can a ____________ ____________ in a ____________?

boat	goat	float

Circle the words that rhyme.
Draw a line to the picture.

1. A fat cat sat
on that hat.

2. Dan can ride
in his tan van.

3. Get the wet pet
out of the net.

4. I wish I had
a fish in a dish.

5. Did you sell the
shell and the bell?

Write the rhyming word.

log	wig	pen	box	vet

1. See the fox in that ______________.

2. A green frog sat on the ______________.

3. Can a pig put on a ______________?

4. I took my pet to see the ______________.

5. Put the hen in her ______________.

Write the rhyming words.

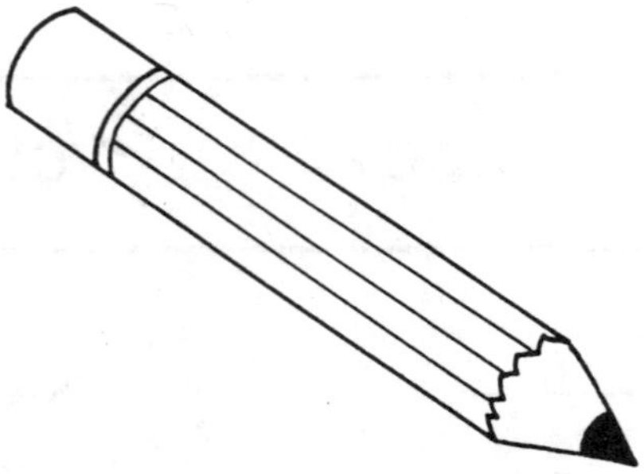

my

sock

jar

pen

three

log

bee	see	hen
by	lock	rock
car	hog	far
fly	frog	ten

Mark the words that rhyme.

hog ~~at~~ oat

Circle the rhyming words.
Color the picture.

a green bug
on a black rug

a red hen
in a brown pen

an orange ball
on a tall wall

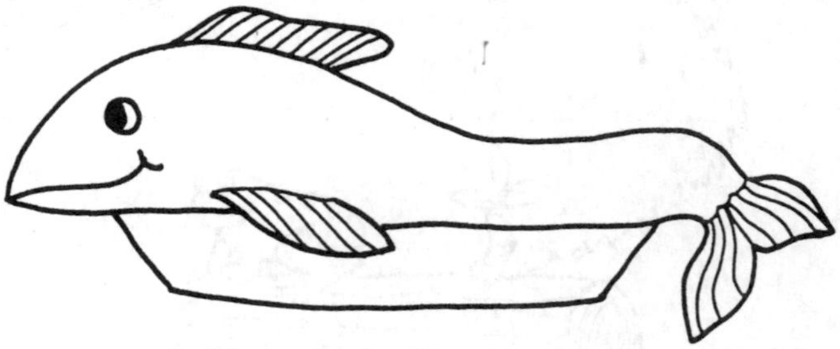

a yellow fish
in a blue dish

Write the rhyming words.

cake	ink	jeep
1.	1.	1.
2.	2.	2.
3.	3.	3.
4.	4.	4.
5.	5.	5.

Color the words that rhyme.

not
down
in

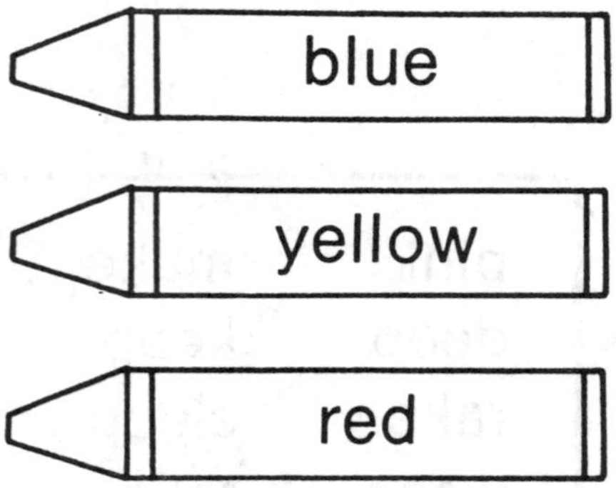

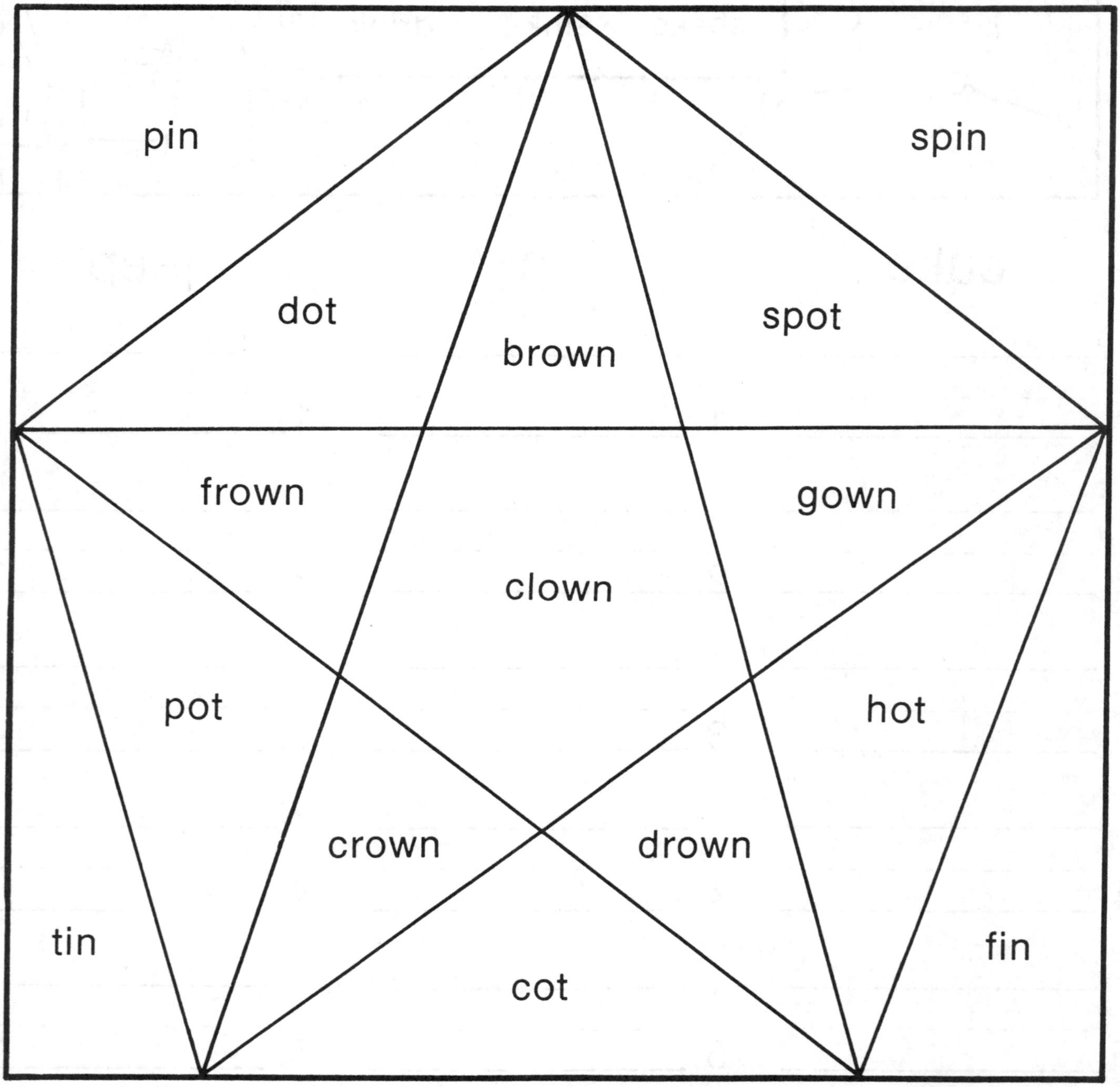

Color the pictures that rhyme.

Finish the word families.

ell

sh___ ___ ___

f___ ___ ___

sp___ ___ ___

w___ ___ ___

t___ ___ ___

ent

t___ ___ ___

r___ ___ ___

b___ ___ ___

d___ ___ ___

s___ ___ ___

ook

b___ ___ ___

l___ ___ ___

cr___ ___ ___

sh___ ___ ___

br___ ___ ___

ail

p___ ___ ___

m___ ___ ___

t___ ___ ___

tr___ ___ ___

qu___ ___ ___

Read the words to a friend.

Riddle Rhymes

Draw

1. I am a fat hog.

2. I am a brown pot.

3. I am a silly rabbit.

4. I am a home for guppies.

bunny	dish	big	fish
tan	pig	pan	funny

Circle the words that rhyme.
Draw the picture.

a hot pot on a red spot	a ball on a tall wall
a tan can in a pan	a wet pet in a net

Write some words that rhyme.

it	an	pot
1. ______	1. ______	1. ______
2. ______	2. ______	2. ______
3. ______	3. ______	3. ______

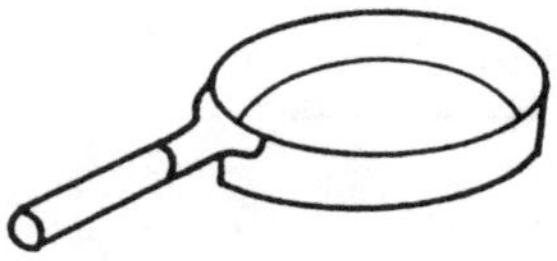

me	bun	get
1. ______	1. ______	1. ______
2. ______	2. ______	2. ______
3. ______	3. ______	3. ______

Fill in the blanks to make rhyming words.

______ar			______ake			
f	______	______	c	______	______	______
c	______	______	r	______	______	______
j	______	______	l	______	______	______
t	______	______	t	______	______	______
st	______	______	sh	______	______	______
______un			**______ all**			
b	______	______	b	______	______	______
f	______	______	c	______	______	______
r	______	______	f	______	______	______
s	______	______	h	______	______	______
g	______	______	t	______	______	______

Match the pictures that rhyme.

ghost

rain

pail

chair

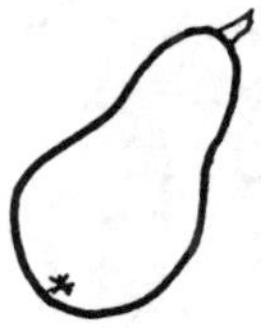

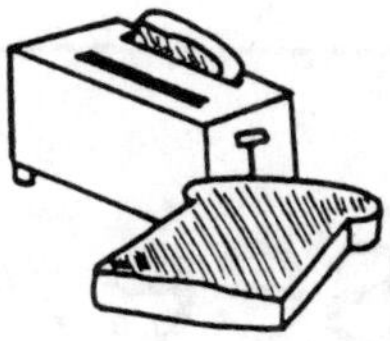

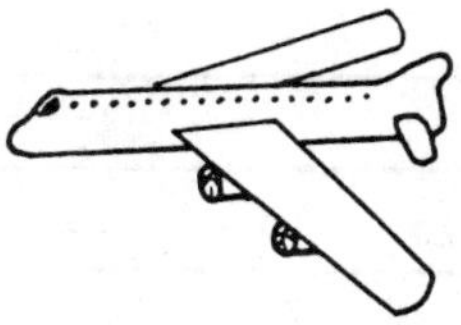

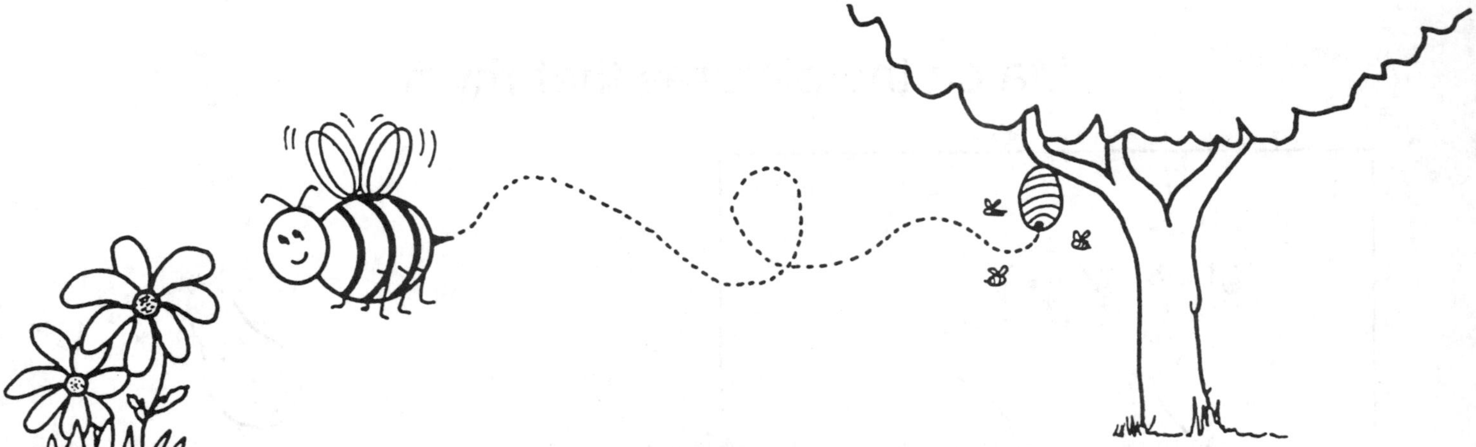

Write the words that rhyme in the boxes.

see	get	zoo

boo	bee	three
bet	shoe	set
we	too	wet
let	he	moo

Write some words that rhyme.

cake	well	down
sock	ink	all

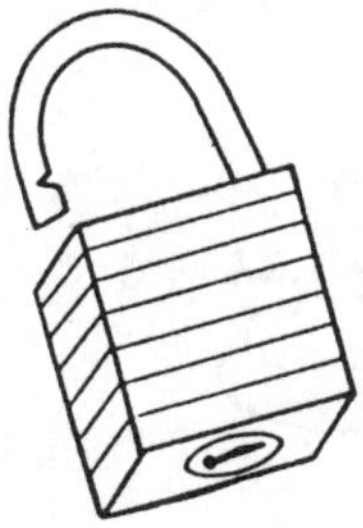   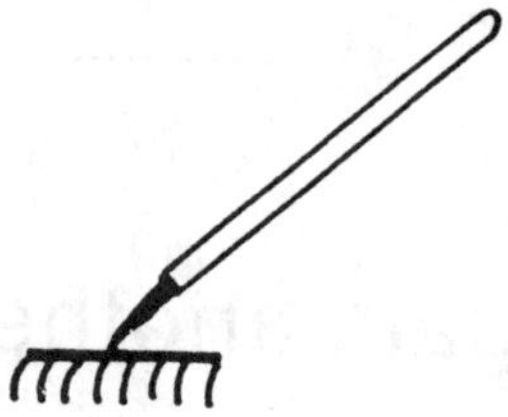 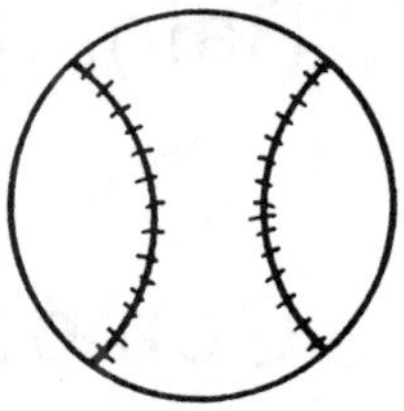

Write the rhyming words.

dock	hill	Muffet	clock	sheep
day	Peep	away	tuffet	Jill

1. Jack and ________

Went up the ________.

2. Little Bo ________

Has lost her ________.

3. Hickory, dickory, ________

The mouse ran up the ________.

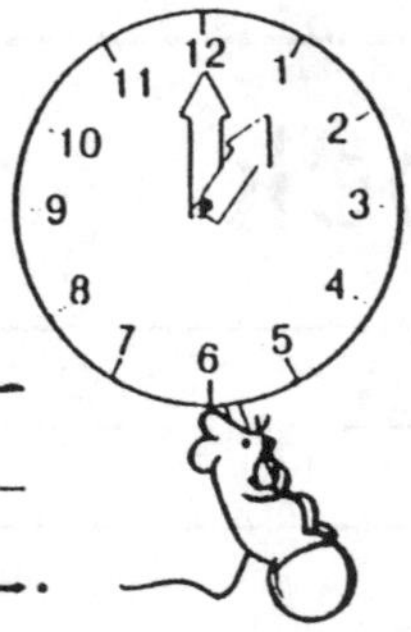

4. Little Miss ________

Sat on a ________.

5. Rain, rain go ________

Come again another ________.

Circle the words that rhyme.
Draw a line to the picture.

1. A mouse ran into the dog house.

2. I think the pink drink is by the sink.

3. Will the ant go up the hill?

4. A black cat is in a sack.

5. A dragon sat on my wagon.

6. I saw the dog's paw.

Color the words that rhyme with:

funny — yellow
day — green
an — blue
back — brown

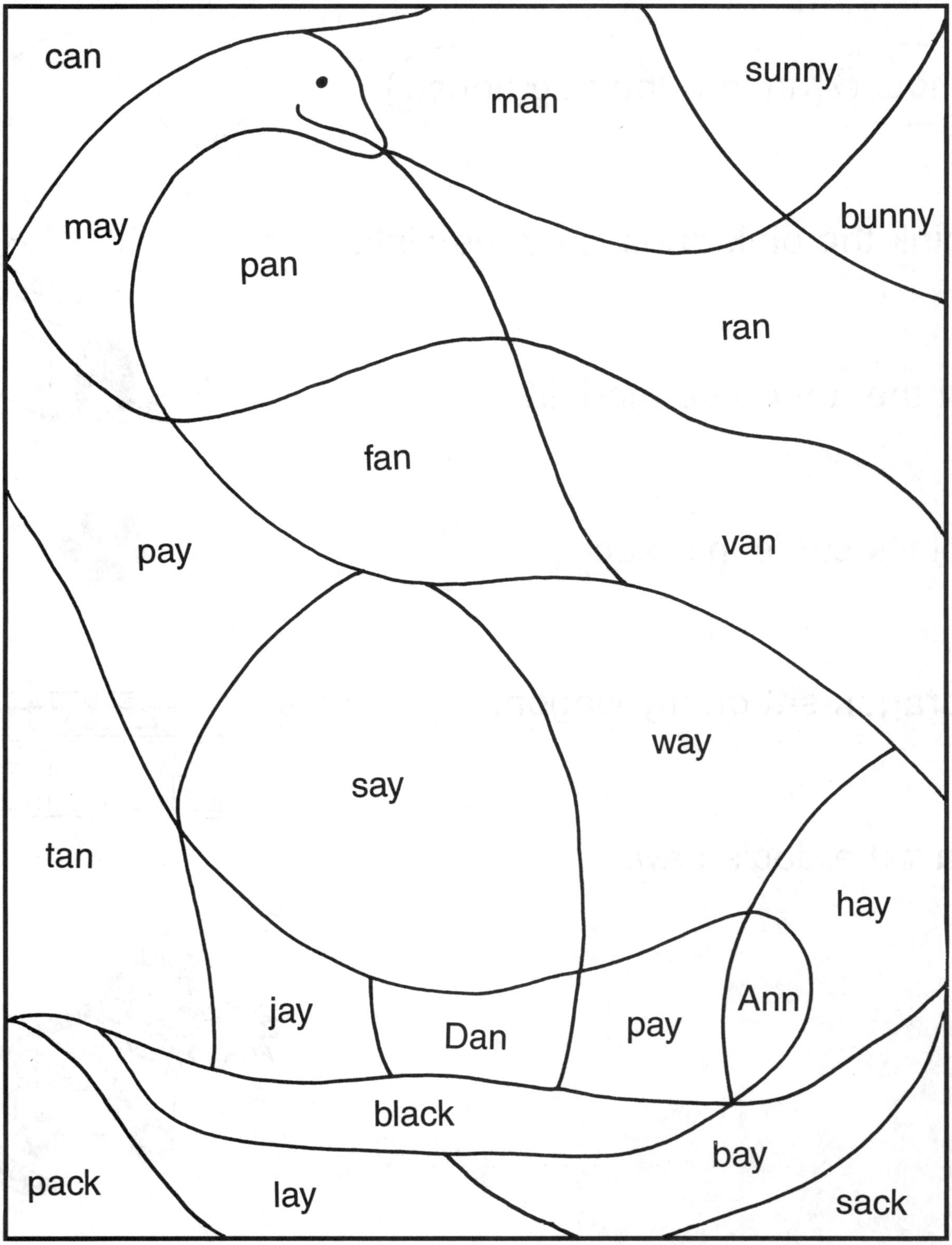

Match the rhyming words:

in	no
take	pin
go	cake
see	sun
bell	goat
run	well
boat	we

Write the rhyming words.

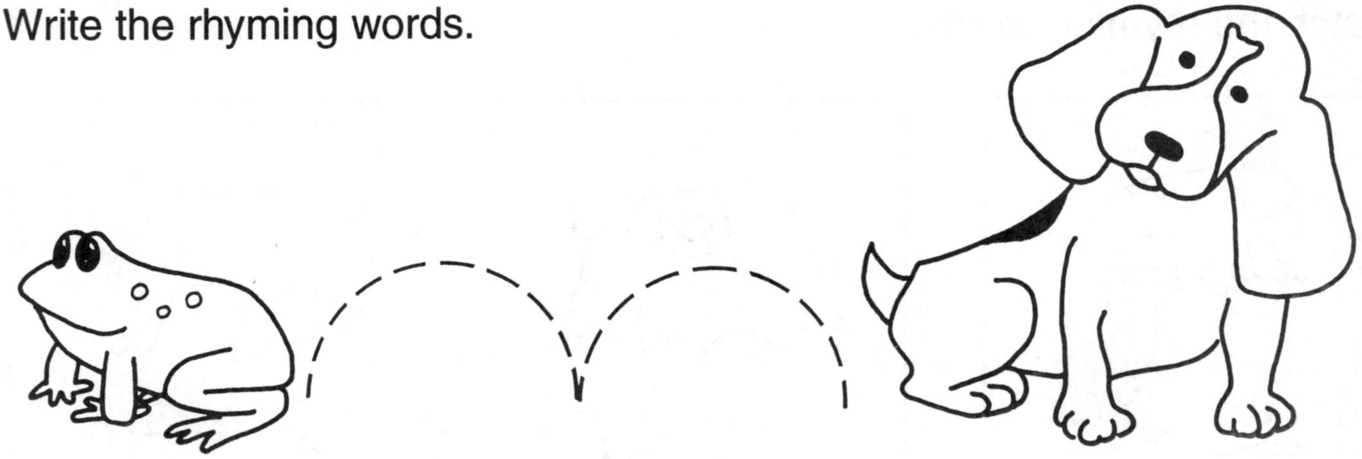

wink

take

top

down

wet

pin

hop	pink	kin	make
tin	town	sink	pet
clown	rake	stop	get

Fill in the blanks using rhyming words.

1. Put the wig

on the pig.

2. He took his ______________________

to see the ______________________.

3. A yellow ______________________

was on the ______________________.

4. I put my ______________________

in the wet ______________________.

5. She ate the ______________________

on that red ______________________.

hand	pig
pet	fish
star	sand
wig	dish
vet	car

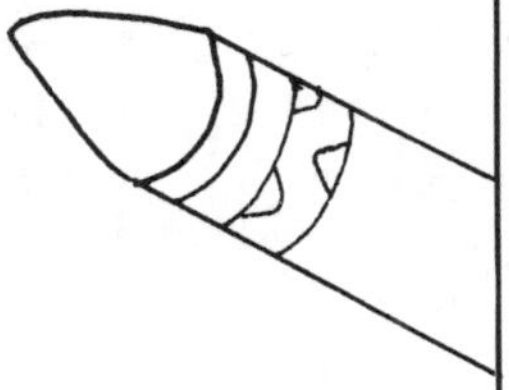

Circle the words that rhyme.
Draw the picture.

A fat bat sat on the red bed.	The tan man had a hot pot.
Put the big pig in a black sack.	A funny bunny hopped on the tall wall.

Answer Key

Please take time to go over the work your child has completed. Ask your child to explain what he/she has done. Praise both success and effort. If mistakes have been made, explain what the answer should have been and how to find it. Let your child know that mistakes are a part of learning. The time you spend with your child helps let him/her know you feel learning is important.

page 1

Finish the words.
ar
far
car
tar
star
en
hen
ten
pen
men
ig
pig
dig
big
wig
an
can
pan
ran
van

page 2

Cut and paste the pictures that rhyme.
3
knee tree bee hat cat rat
hoe snow toe frown gown clown

page 3

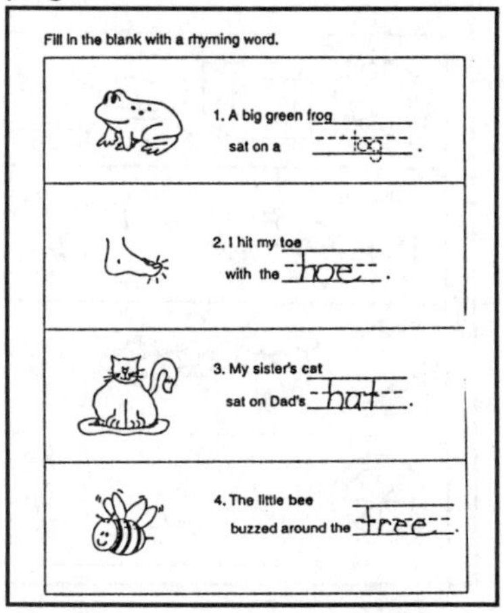
Fill in the blank with a rhyming word.
1. A big green frog sat on a log.
2. I hit my toe with the hoe.
3. My sister's cat sat on Dad's hat.
4. The little bee buzzed around the tree.

page 4

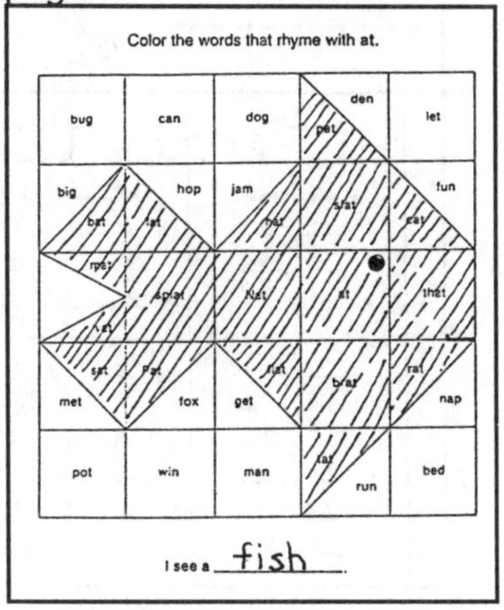
Color the words that rhyme with at.
bug can dog den let
big hop jam fun
bat sat hat cat
mat fat Nat at that
sat Pat bat rat
met fox get nap
pot win man tat run bed
I see a fish.

page 5

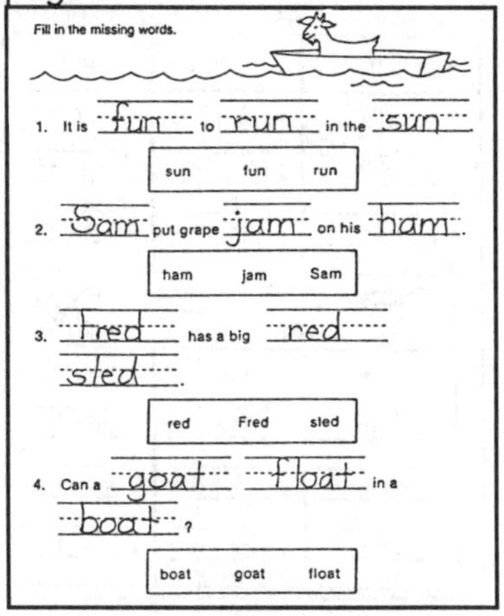
Fill in the missing words.
1. It is fun to run in the sun.
sun fun run
2. Sam put grape jam on his ham.
ham jam Sam
3. Fred has a big red sled.
red Fred sled
4. Can a goat float in a boat?
boat goat float

page 6

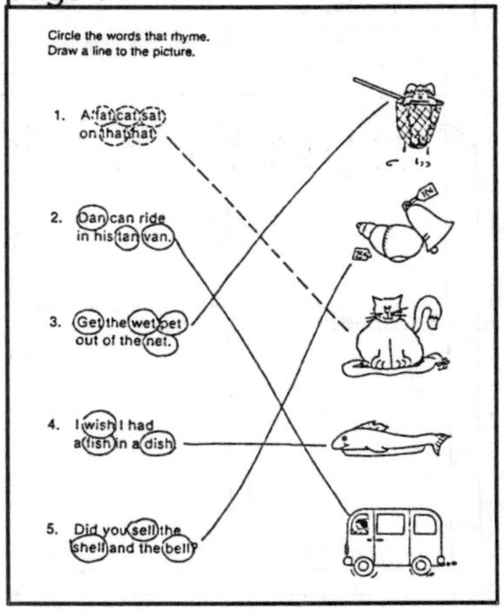
Circle the words that rhyme.
Draw a line to the picture.
1. A fat cat sat on that hat.
2. Dan can ride in his tan van.
3. Get the wet pet out of the net.
4. I wish I had a fish in a dish.
5. Did you sell the shell and the bell?

page 7

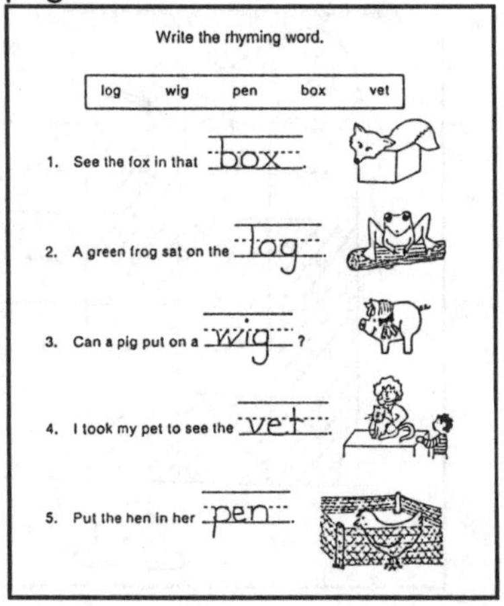
Write the rhyming word.
log wig pen box vet
1. See the fox in that box.
2. A green frog sat on the log.
3. Can a pig put on a wig?
4. I took my pet to see the vet.
5. Put the hen in her pen.

page 8

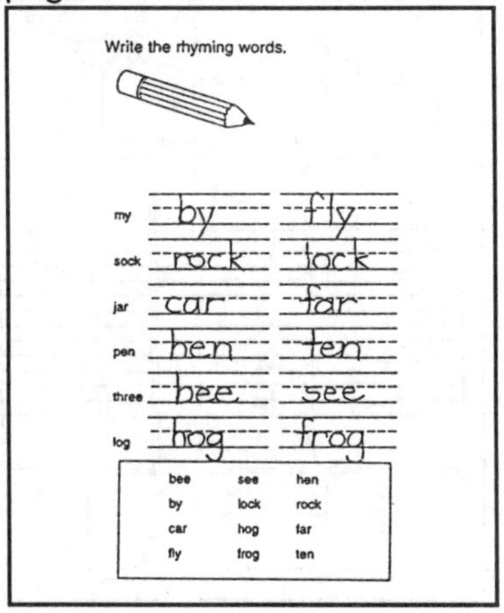
Write the rhyming words.
my by fly
sock rock lock
jar car far
pen hen ten
three bee see
log hog frog
bee see hen
by lock rock
car hog far
fly frog ten

page 9

Mark the words that rhyme.
hog
at
oat

page 10

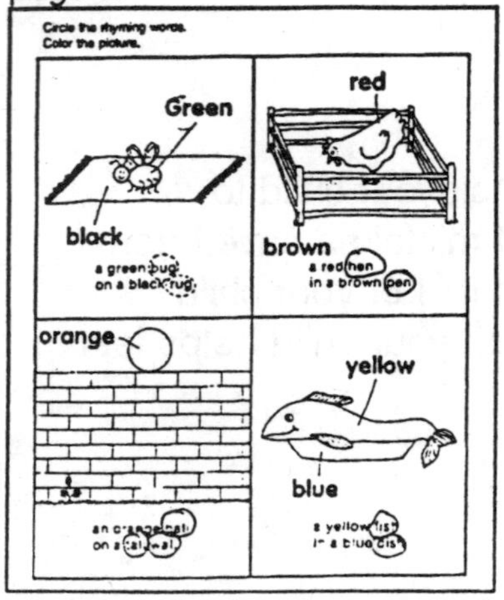

page 11

page 12

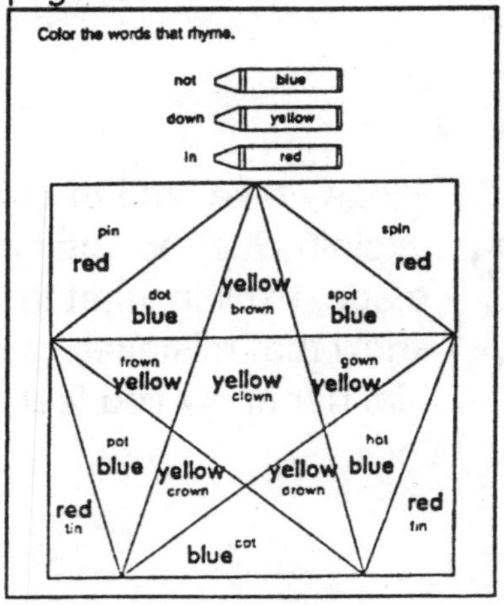

page 13

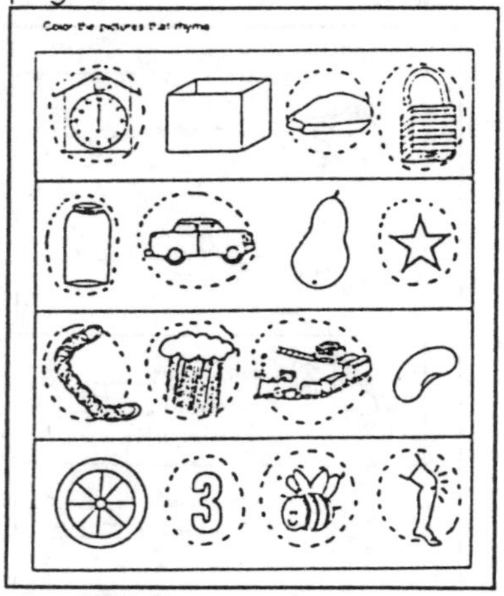

page 14

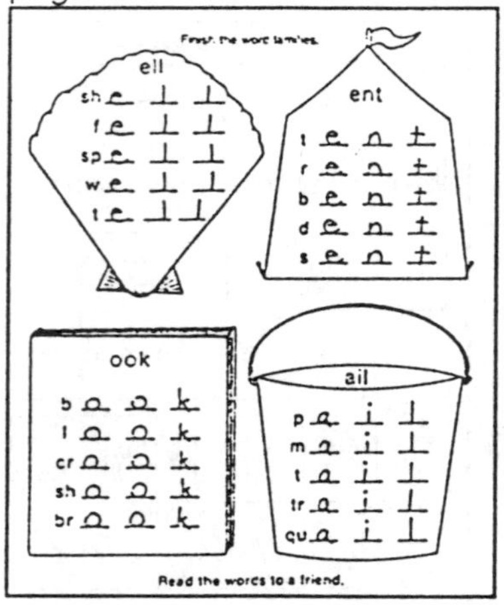

page 15

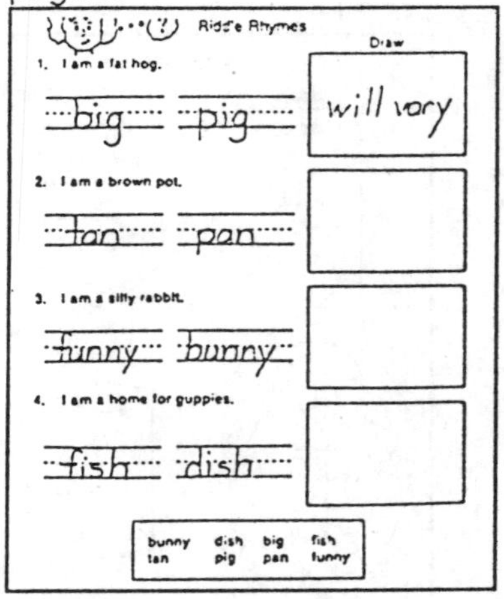

page 16

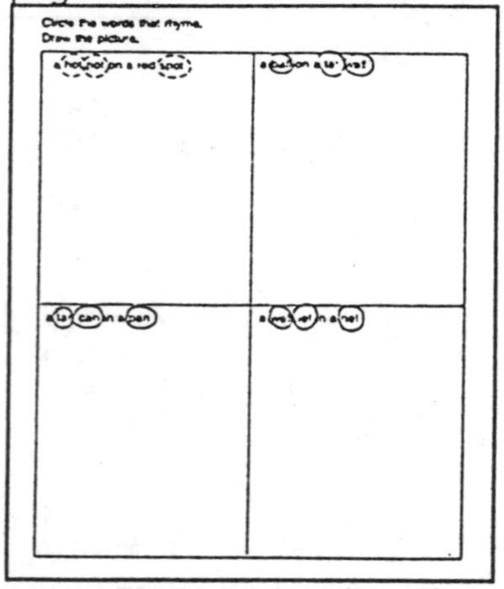

page 17

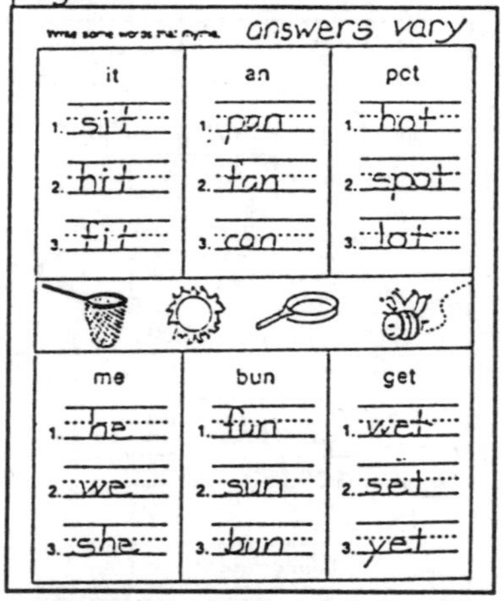

page 18

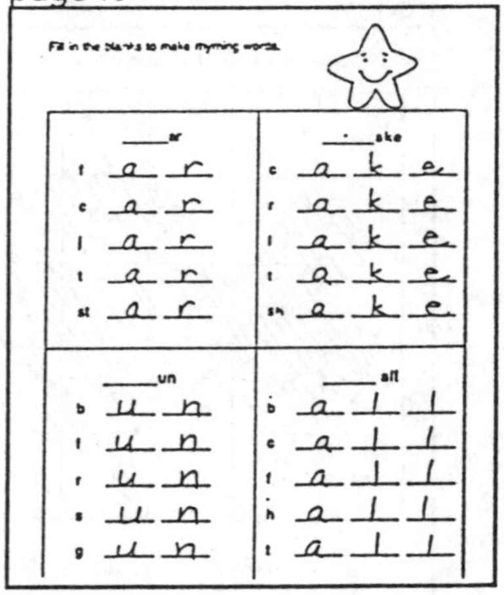

page 19

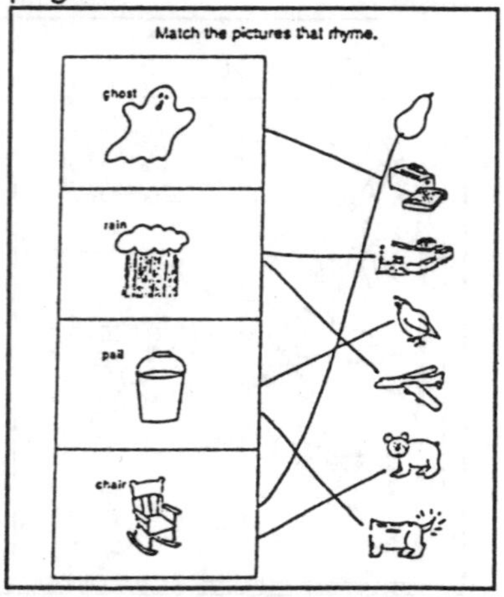

page 20

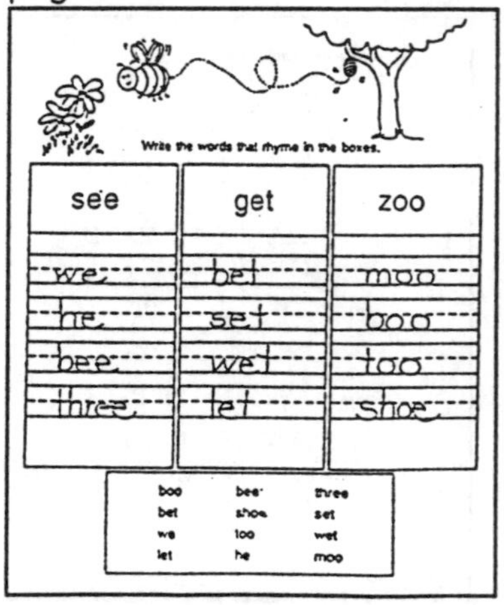

page 21

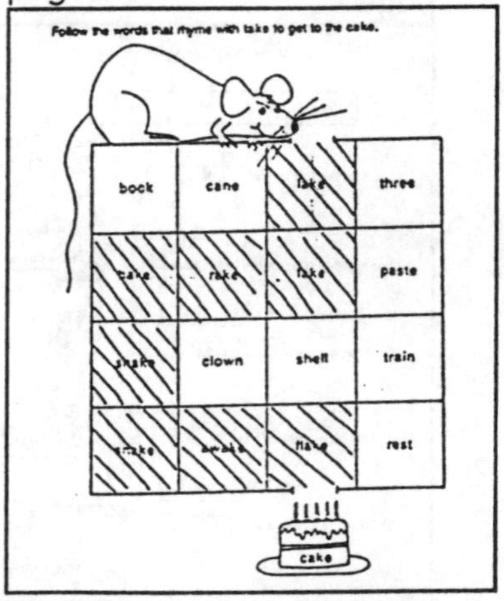